stillness, silence, solitude

TIME
WITH
God

Reflections on the Psalms, 1-18

RONALD L. DART

Wasteland Press
Shelbyville, KY USA
www.wastelandpress.net

Time with God, Reflections on the Psalms, 1-18
by Ronald L. Dart

Copyright © 2007 Ronald L. Dart
ALL RIGHTS RESERVED

First Printing – November 2007
ISBN: 978-1-60047-149-0

Unless otherwise indicated, All Scripture citations are the King James
Version, paraphrased, others as indicated in the text:

NASB: Scripture quotations taken from the New American Standard
Bible®, Copyright © 1960, 1962, 1963, 1968, 1971,1972, 1973, 1975,
1977, 1995 by The Lockman Foundation. Used by permission.
(www.Lockman.org)

NIV: Scripture taken from the HOLY BIBLE, NEW INTERNATIONAL
VERSION®. Copyright © 1973, 1978, 1984 International Bible
Society. Used by permission of Zondervan. All rights reserved.

Printed in the U.S.A.

Prologue

Many years ago when I was having trouble praying, I found an approach that turned my prayer life around. It may have even turned my life around. I don't know if someone suggested it to me, or if I discovered it on my own. But it grew out of an attempt to spend more time with God in prayer when I didn't really have an awful lot to say.

What I did was to pray as long as I could and then, while still on my knees and with my Bible open before me, I started to read the first Psalm and talk to God about it. When I finished, I put a mark in my Bible and went on to Psalm 2. I have two old Bibles, and I have gone through both of them doing this—several times each.

Then, a few years ago, I thought about people whose lives are so busy they find themselves on the go all the time, with very little time for meditation. So I went to the studio and with the help of Gary Gibbons, made a recording of the Psalms along with my reflections on each of them. This book is an updated version of those readings, for people who would rather curl up with a book than listen to a CD (I tend to fall in this class myself). Bear in mind that my purpose in this book is not argument, not polemics, but simply time with God.

I suggest that you pause at the end of each Psalm to think about it for a while. If you are a bedtime reader, the Psalms make a fine source of meditation after you turn out the lights. This book will mean the most to you if you spend some time in thought after each Psalm. You will remember it longer and it will mean more to you.

People often ask me what translation I am using when I speak. I work from the old King James Bible, partly because it just has better style, but mainly because of long familiarity. When I started reading the Bible, the King James was the only Bible I knew. Consequently, all my memories of Scripture are in the King James. At the same time, I paraphrase it as I go. Let's face it, the old version is a little hard to read aloud and it falls strangely on the modern ear.

That, coupled with the fact that the KJV is in public domain, led me to use my own paraphrase of that great old Bible in this book. I will provide footnotes where explanation is needed.

1

I hope you will keep a pencil at hand as you read. If you don't mind marking a book, you are likely to find occasion to add your own reflections in the margins. Some of my best ideas come as I read, but if I don't make a note, they are apt to get away from me. And maybe you will even want to drop me a note with your reflections and thoughts. They will be most welcome.

You will notice that I have rendered the Psalms in lines rather than paragraphs. The Psalms were written as music, albeit music strange to our ears. The eight note scale had not yet been invented. I have shaped the Psalms to convey transitions and to make them easier to read aloud. Most of the ancients would never have seen these Psalms on the printed page. Even if they were literate, it is doubtful that many could afford to have their own scrolls. Mostly, they heard the Psalms read aloud, again and again, and they memorized many of them as a part of their education. Since the invention of printing, we have all but lost the art of memorization.

If you have friends or family who are agreeable, I suggest you try reading the Psalms aloud to each other, shaping them verbally with pacing and emphasis. There is much more meaning in these pages than the printed word. If you prefer, I have read all 150 Psalms for an audio album which is available from Christian Educational Ministries at the address, phone number, or website below.

Christian Educational Ministries
P.O. Box 560
Whitehouse, TX 75791
1-888-BIBLE-44
www.borntowin.net

Psalm 1

Blessed is the man who walks
not in the counsel of the ungodly,
nor stands in the way of sinners,
nor sits in the seat of the scornful.
But his delight is in the law of the LORD;
and in his law does he meditate day and night.
3
He shall be like a tree planted by the rivers of water,
that brings forth his fruit in his season;
his leaf also shall not wither
and whatever he does shall prosper.
4
The ungodly are not so:
but are like the chaff which the wind drives away.
Therefore the ungodly shall not stand in the judgment,
nor sinners in the assembly of the righteous.
For the LORD knows the way of the righteous:
but the way of the ungodly shall perish.

There are 150 Psalms. Why was this one placed first? It isn't everyone's favorite. The 23rd Psalm takes that honor. I think it is here because it sets the tone for the work to follow: It is a winner's formula for life. There are two important principles that make all the difference: (1) You don't take counsel of a certain class of men. (2) You make the law of God your counselor, your tutor, the teacher of your conscience.

The law of God is not a yoke of bondage, nor is it shackles and chains. It is a lamp to our feet and a light to our path. The law of God is a descriptor of what works in life. The man who internalizes it gains an edge. Men will study books day and night that they think will

La ley de Dios es 3 como una lampara
a nuestros pies y una luz para nuestra
boveda

give them an edge in the stock market. They do it for money. The law of God gives a man an edge in *everything*.

The law can be a painful study because we break it so often. It is not that we *can't* keep the law in any one of its parts or on any given occasion. We can do that. But keeping it perfectly all the time is rather beyond most of us. Superficially, the law seems complicated, but that is only because the law is about life. It is *life* that is complicated. So when we study the law, and "meditate on it day and night," we routinely come across mistakes we have made. There is no gain in agonizing over past mistakes. The gain is in recognizing them and correcting them. The grace of God is what allows us to use the law without being discouraged by it.

The stock market makes a good analogy; we do not feel guilty when we make a mistake investing. We cut our losses and try not to make the same mistake again. When we study the law of God, we *do* feel guilty. Yet, what God is after is not guilt, but change. What he wants us to do is learn from our mistakes and not repeat them. It's called repentance.

"The LORD knows the way of the righteous," is a curious expression. The word "know" is the Hebrew word *yada* which is also used in Genesis 4:1, "And Adam *knew* Eve his wife; and she conceived, and bare Cain." It is also the root of the word for "knowledge" in "The tree of the knowledge of good and evil." So it means rather more than "knowing about" something.

Words often come to have special meanings beyond their denotation. For example, we can say that we hope a person will not see adversity or know pain. In both cases, the verb has to do, not merely with seeing or knowing, but about *experiencing*. So when the Psalm tells us "the LORD knows the way of the righteous" it is saying something more than merely that he watches us walk that way. Some versions render the phrase, "The Lord watches over the way of the righteous." It is more than that. The Lord knows our way because he has walked in it.

This Psalm also serves as a good introduction to poetic structure. The psalmist could have said, "Blessed is the man who is neither ungodly, a sinner, or scornful." Instead, he chooses the poetic way of saying it. Whether we are walking, standing, or sitting, we must not

4

conform to these patterns of life. Hebrew poetry comes through in translation, because it doesn't depend on rhyme. It is a poetry of ideas.

At the end, the psalmist returns to his opening theme but gathers all the contrasting ways of life into one: the ungodly. First, we are led to understand the benefits of walking in God's law, and then we turn to the consequences of the ungodly way of life.

Scornful: It occurs to me that one needs to be very careful in the use of satire, especially if the audience is not in on the joke. Satire has an angry undercurrent, and it is easy to slip over the line into scorn.

About the name, Jehovah: In that day, other gods were a constant presence, even a threat, so it was important to identify whose law the psalmist was talking about. The convention, followed by nearly every version of the Bible, is to substitute the word LORD in small caps wherever the Hebrew *YHWH* is found. This is acceptable as far as it goes, but there are places in the Psalms where it is important to know that God is personal and has a name. Scholars use *Yahweh*, the Hebrew name, instead of "Jehovah," the name in English. I use Jehovah when it is important to emphasize the name because nearly every reader will recognize it.

About meditation: We are so blessed in this generation. Through most of human history, meditation on the law required memorization, something that earlier generations were much better at than we. We can carry a Bible with us wherever we go, and we can even load it up on a Blackberry. The problem is that something so readily available is neglected because "I can have that anytime." It is not as precious to us as it might be, and thus requires a different kind of discipline.

About the phrase, "That brings forth his fruit in his season": I sometimes find myself troubled at a lack of results, and yet here is a hint that fruit only comes in its season. A tree is quiet in the winter, yet the roots keep water flowing, and the work of winter is done internally and underground. In the spring, the leaves come forth, and in the summer the fruit begins to appear. Patience is often in short supply in the modern world, but I find it helpful to be reminded that I don't have to bear fruit all the time—only in season.

Psalm 2

Why do the heathen rage,
and the people imagine a vain thing?
The kings of the earth set themselves,
and the rulers take counsel together,
against Jehovah, and against his anointed,
saying, Let us break their bands asunder,
and cast away their cords from us.

4

He that sits in the heavens shall laugh:
the Lord shall have them in derision.
Then shall he speak unto them in his wrath,
and vex them in his sore displeasure.

6

Yet have I set my king upon my holy hill of Zion.
I will declare the decree: Jehovah has said unto me,
You art my Son; this day have I begotten you.
Ask of me, and I shall give you the heathen
for your inheritance, and the uttermost parts of the earth
for your possession.
You shall break them with a rod of iron;
You shall dash them in pieces like a potter's vessel.

10

Be wise now therefore, O ye kings:
be instructed, ye judges of the earth.
Serve Jehovah with fear,
and rejoice with trembling.
Kiss the Son, lest he be angry,
and ye perish from the way,
when his wrath is kindled but a little.
Blessed are all they that put their trust in him.

One has to wonder what the author of the second Psalm thought it meant. It may have been written at a time when Israel's hegemony was being challenged by the surrounding nations. David had expanded Israel's borders and oversaw something of an empire. We know that David and his men prevailed against his neighbors every time they challenged him.

But it is plain enough as one reads forward that there is rather more to the Psalm than that. It goes messianic immediately. The expression, "You are my Son; this day have I begotten you," can apply to David, but only in metaphor. The verse is cited twice in Hebrews and there applied to Jesus (Hebrews 1:5 and 5:5). So, it is plain enough that we are dealing with a messianic Psalm.

The glorified Jesus made reference to this Psalm in a letter to the church at Thyatira.

> And he that overcomes, and keeps my works unto the end, to him will I give power over the nations: And he shall rule them with a rod of iron; as the vessels of a potter shall they be broken to shivers: *even as I received of my Father* (Revelation 2:26-27).

In the Psalm, "the Son" seems clearly a reference to Jesus, the Son of God who is to rule the whole world. The author of the Psalm may have thought of David, but the idea of the *Son* is transcendent. This underlines a curious thing about the Psalms. They aren't just religious poetry or music. Many of them are highly prophetic, looking all the way down to the last days.

The music of the Psalms would fall strangely on our ears. David and others used stringed instruments, but the musical scale we use was still far in the future. Apparently they had ten strings—ten tones to work with.

I'm struck with the fact that, in the ancient world, when a nation went to war, they went to war with the opposing nation's *god*. It was not merely king against king, but god against god. This explains why the men of Israel carried the Ark of the Testimony into battle against the Philistines. And this is how we should understand the opening stanza of this Psalm: "the rulers take counsel together, against *Jehovah*, and against his anointed." It is, in fact, god against God.

Psalm 3

A Psalm of David,
when he fled from Absalom his son.

Lᴏʀᴅ, how are they increased that trouble me!
many are they that rise up against me.
Many there be which say of my soul,
There is no help for him in God. [Pause.]
3
But you, O Lᴏʀᴅ, are a shield for me;
my glory, and the lifter up of my head.
I cried unto the Lᴏʀᴅ with my voice,
and he heard me out of his holy hill. [Pause.]
I laid me down and slept; I awoke;
for the Lᴏʀᴅ sustained me.
I will not be afraid of ten thousands of people,
that have set themselves against me round about.
7
Arise, O Lᴏʀᴅ; save me, O my God:
for you have smitten all my enemies
upon the cheek bone;
you have broken the teeth of the ungodly.
Salvation belongs unto the Lᴏʀᴅ:
your blessing is upon your people. [Pause.]

This is the first Psalm that is a prayer. Psalm 1 is an exhortation, while the second is more of a prophecy. Now we come to a man who is deeply stressed, who cries out to God for help.

If the superscription on this Psalm is correct, it came at one of the lowest periods of David's life. The attempted coup by Absalom, David's son, and David's flight from Jerusalem is one of the most poignant stories in the Bible. The fear and dread of a palace coup must have been compounded by the fact that his enemy was his own son. One wonders if David would have fled before anyone else, or if he would have stayed and fought.

"I will not be afraid of ten thousands of people, that have set themselves against me," he wrote. And yet he fled Jerusalem. Why?

I think of this Psalm as having been written before David knew how the coup would finally play out. One of the most heartbreaking choral works I have ever heard is a rendering of the words of David upon hearing of the death of Absalom. Mind you, his son was a rebel who had sent David running from Jerusalem for his life. After a great battle between David's men and those of Absalom, David learned of the death of Absalom. The song is called, "David's Lament," and it is an almost verbatim rendering of the words in Scripture: "And the king was much moved, and went to his chamber and wept: and as he went, he wept and said, O my son Absalom, my son, my son Absalom! would God I had died for thee, O Absalom, my son, my son!" (2 Samuel 18:33).

David was a man after God's own heart, and nothing would have pleased him more than if his son had repented and turned to him. I think David fled Jerusalem, not from fear of battle. I think he fled because he feared that he would have to kill his son. He was willing to face exile, even death, rather than see the death of his son, enemy though Absalom had become.

> But God commends his love toward us,
> in that, while we were yet sinners,
> Christ died for us (Romans 5:8).

> Would God I had died for thee,
> O Absalom, my son, my son.

9

Psalm 4

To the chief Musician on strings,
A Psalm of David.

Hear me when I call,
O God of my righteousness:
you gave me room when I was in distress;
have mercy upon me, and hear my prayer.
2
O ye sons of men,
how long will ye turn my honor into shame?
how long will ye love vanity, and pursue lying? [1]
But know that the LORD has set apart
him that is kind for himself:
the LORD will hear when I call unto him.
Stand in awe, and sin not:
commune with your own heart upon your bed,
and be still. [Pause.]
5
Offer the sacrifices of righteousness,
and put your trust in the LORD.
There be many that say,
Who will show us any good?
LORD, lift up the light of your countenance upon us.
You have put gladness in my heart, more than
in the time that their corn and their wine increased.
8
I will both lay me down in peace, and sleep:
for you, LORD, only make me dwell in safety.

---

[1] Hebrew: *kazab*, "falsehood."

Psalm 4 presents the leader of a great country, blessed by God. A man whose greatest accomplishments are made out to be shameful by his enemies. Their aim was deception. They yapped at his heels like a pack of dogs. But he tells himself to stand in awe of God and to avoid becoming like the men who hated him.

This Psalm seems to come during hard times. There are many who say, "Who will show us any good?" Nothing is going right. But the psalmist says that he has more gladness in heart than they do when everything is going great. The economy being agriculture, this has probably been a bad year.

What does it take to be happy when things are going bad? Sometimes it takes a broader vision, a different perspective. There was a day when Elisha and his servant were in a city besieged by a huge army.

And when the servant of the man of God was risen early, and gone forth, behold, an host compassed the city both with horses and chariots. And his servant said unto him, Alas, my master! how shall we do? And he answered, Fear not: for they that be with us are more than they that be with them. And Elisha prayed, and said, LORD, I pray you, *open his eyes, that he may see.* And the LORD opened the eyes of the young man; and he saw: and, behold, the mountain was full of horses and chariots of fire round about Elisha (2 Kings 6:15-17).

Sometimes we just can't see. That doesn't mean the chariots of fire aren't there. So we make a conscious decision to trust God, no matter what is there. Like the three Hebrew children facing the fiery furnace told the king, "Our God will deliver us from the furnace, O king. But even if not, we will *still* not bow down to your image."

There is a reason why this Psalm seems so apt to our own age, our own leadership, our own people. The jealousy of power is a human constant, and it corrupts men in every age. Technology increases power, but it doesn't change human nature a whit. That conscious decision to trust God, come hell or high water, is what we call, "faith." It is not a feeling. It is a decision made in *defiance* of feeling.

11

Psalm 5

To the chief Musician upon flutes,
A Psalm of David.

𝕲𝖎𝖛𝖊 ear to my words, O LORD,
consider my meditation.
Hearken to the voice of my cry,
my King, and my God: for unto you will I pray.
My voice shall you hear in the morning, O LORD;
in the morning will I direct my prayer unto you,
and I will watch.
4
For you are not a God that has pleasure in wickedness:
neither shall evil dwell with you.
The foolish shall not stand in your sight:
you hate all workers of iniquity.
You shalt destroy them that speak lying:
the LORD will abhor the bloody and deceitful man.
7
But as for me, I will come into thy house
in the multitude of thy mercy:
and in thy fear will I worship toward thy holy temple.
Lead me, O LORD, in thy righteousness
because of my enemies;
make your way straight before my face.
For there is no faithfulness in their mouth;
their inward part is very wickedness;
their throat is an open sepulcher;
they flatter with their tongue.
10
Destroy them, O God;
let them fall by their own counsels;
cast them out in the multitude of their transgressions;

For they have rebelled against you.
But let all those that put their trust in you rejoice:
let them ever shout for joy, because you defend them:
let them also that love your name be joyful in you.
For you, LORD, wilt bless the righteous;
with favor wilt you compass him as with a shield.

In our generation, we are no strangers to the bloody and deceitful man. It seems certain that while technology changes, evil remains always the same. If anything has changed it is that bloody and deceitful men can kill more people than at any time in the history of man.

It seems likely that David had a particular bloody and deceitful man in mind when he wrote this. Reading so many centuries later, we generalize, but David is not generalizing when he speaks of his enemies. When we read the story of Absalom, the flattery, the unfaithfulness becomes especially painful.

But there is an interesting aside here. David never names anyone in his prayers asking God to punish the wicked. One wonders if this is to avoid judging the men in question. We never know all the facts in a case, and there may be mitigating circumstances. We may think a man is lying when he really is not. Therefore to pray against that man would be wrong, while praying that God will punish the unnamed liar would be fair. If the man is innocent, the curse will not come. It is a singular evil to curse an innocent man. David prayed against his enemies without naming them. Thus, if a man really was not his enemy, David had done no harm. "As the bird by wandering, as the swallow by flying, so the curse causeless shall not come" (Proverbs 26:2).

Psalm 6

To the Chief Musician upon the Lyre,
A Psalm of David.

O LORD, rebuke me not in your anger,
neither chasten me in your hot displeasure.
Have mercy upon me, O LORD, for I am weak:
O LORD, heal me; for my bones tremble.[1]
My soul also trembles:
but you, O LORD, how long?

4

Return, O LORD, deliver my soul:
oh save me for thy mercies' sake.
For in death there is no remembrance of you:
in the grave who shall give you thanks?

6

I am weary with my groaning;
all the night make I my bed to swim;
I water my couch with my tears.
Mine eye is consumed because of grief;
it waxes old because of all mine enemies.

8

Depart from me, all ye workers of iniquity;
for the LORD has heard the voice of my weeping.
The LORD has heard my supplication;
the LORD will receive my prayer.
Let all mine enemies be ashamed and tremble:
let them turn back and be suddenly ashamed.

---

[1] Hebrew: *bahal*, "to tremble inwardly."

I suppose everyone has nights like this—nights when we are sore afraid of God's displeasure—for it is hard for a man to make it through this life without encountering shame and fear. On this night, David feared for his life, and he had more than a few nights like this. He bargained with God just a little: "In death there is no remembrance of you," he said, "in the grave who shall give you thanks? Of what little use I am, Lord, it is better than being dead."

And yet in his darkest hours, David never lost hope. "Get away from me, you lawless louts," he cries. "God has heard me. He will receive my prayer."

The one who accuses us before God, though, is not a man. It is a spirit who is called, "the accuser of our brethren." [1] "Get away from me, O my enemy. God has heard my prayer."

Psalm 7

*Improvisation [2] of David,
which he sang unto the LORD,
concerning the words of
Cush the Benjamite.*

O LORD my God, in you do I put my trust:
save me from all them that persecute me, and deliver me:
Lest he tear my soul like a lion,
rending it in pieces, while there is none to deliver.

3

O LORD my God, if I have done this;
if there be iniquity in my hands;
If I have rewarded evil unto him
that was at peace with me;
(yea, I have delivered him

---

[1] Revelation 12:10.

[2] Hebrew, *Shiggaion*, meaning "irregular," i.e., a rambling poem.

that without cause is mine enemy:)
Let the enemy persecute my soul, and take it;
yea, let him tread down my life upon the earth,
and lay mine honor in the dust. (Pause).

6

Arise, O LORD, in thine anger,
lift up yourself because of the rage of mine enemies:
and awake for me to the judgment
that you have appointed.
So shall the assembly of the people surround you:
for their sakes therefore return you on high.

8

The LORD shall judge the people:
judge me, O LORD, according to my righteousness,
and according to mine integrity that is in me.
Oh let the wickedness of the wicked come to an end;
but establish the just:
for the righteous God tries the hearts and reins.

10

My defense is of God, who saves the upright in heart.
God judges the righteous,
and God is angry with the wicked every day.
If the wicked turn not, he will whet his sword;
he has bent his bow, and made it ready.
He has also prepared for him the instruments of death;
he ordains his arrows against the persecutors.
Behold, the persecutor is bound with iniquity,
and has conceived mischief,
and brought forth falsehood.
He made a pit, and digged it,
and is fallen into the ditch which he made.
His mischief shall return upon his own head,
and his violent dealing shall come down upon his own pate.

17

I will praise the LORD according to his righteousness:
and will sing praise to the name of the LORD most high.

It takes courage to ask God to "judge me according to my righteousness." It was especially so for a man like David whose unrighteousness was so well documented. I can only conclude that David knew he had been forgiven of his sins and that his iniquity was no longer attributed to him. When God says he will no longer remember a person's iniquity, he must mean it quite literally.[1] God looks on the heart, and when the past is truly past, he will not hold it against us. At the same time, when a man makes this his prayer, it has a curious way of calling him up short and making him realize that his conduct matters.

There's another line that should make us think: "Oh let the wickedness of the wicked come to an end." This is an interesting thought. He does not call for the end of the wicked, but for the wickedness of the wicked. It may be a distinction without a difference, but maybe not. Surely it can inform our own prayers about the actions of wicked people.

The superscription on this Psalm reads: A *Shiggaion* of David, which he sang unto the LORD, concerning the words of Cush the Benjamite." It is uncertain who is after David. Some say the name "Cush" is an epithet applied to Shimei,[2] one of the sons of Saul. If so, then the event was David's flight before his own son, Absalom. The accusation was that David was a bloody man and was responsible for the death of Saul and Jonathan. David could rightly say that he had not done this. He had, in fact, delivered Saul on more than one occasion when he could have killed him.

---

[1] Isaiah 43:25.

[2] See 2 Samuel 16:7 ff.

17

Psalm 8

To the chief Musician upon the harp
A Psalm of David.

O LORD our Lord,
how excellent is your name in all the earth!
You have set your glory above the heavens.
Out of the mouth of babes and sucklings
have you ordained strength because of thine enemies,
that you might still the enemy and the avenger.

3

When I consider your heavens, the work of your fingers,
the moon and the stars, which you have ordained;
What is man, that you are mindful of him?
and the son of man, that you visit him?
For you have made him a little lower than the angels,
and have crowned him with glory and honor.
You made him to have dominion
over the works of your hands;
you have put all things under his feet:
All sheep and oxen, yea, and the beasts of the field;
The fowl of the air, and the fish of the sea,
and whatsoever passes through the paths of the seas.

9

O LORD our Lord,
how excellent is your name in all the earth!

The Psalmist is awestruck. A clear, dark, moonless night can do that to a man. There is so much light pollution these days, that very few ever see anything like the sky David saw camped out far away from Jerusalem. I remember the sky I saw in my childhood on the farm, but I had to go to sea to experience that in recent years. One night, sailing back to Galveston from Mexico, I was off watch and asleep when a voice called down and woke me. "Come

18

up here, Ron, you have to see this." I went topside and saw a sky I had not seen in years. But not for long. Shortly, the moon began to make a show of rising in the east, making magic with a few clouds on the horizon. I'll never forget it.

David could not possibly know the true vastness of the universe, but he could see enough to know how small he was. It is in understanding how small I am that I can appreciate what it means to know that God is with me. When Paul wrote Hebrews, he could still see that sky, and he called it as a witness:

> But there is a place where someone has testified: "What is man that you are mindful of him, the son of man that you care for him? You made him a little lower than the angels; you crowned him with glory and honor and put everything under his feet." In putting everything under him, God left nothing that is not subject to him. Yet at present we do not see everything subject to him. But we see Jesus, who was made a little lower than the angels, now crowned with glory and honor because he suffered death, so that by the grace of God he might taste death for everyone. In bringing many sons to glory, it was fitting that God, for whom and through whom everything exists, should make the author of their salvation perfect through suffering (Hebrews 2:6-10 NIV).

But David saw enough to make him sing: "O LORD our Lord, how excellent is your name in all the earth!" It sounds poetic, but that isn't what David wrote. The original is, "O *Jehovah* our Lord, how excellent is your *name* in all the earth." This isn't to say that there is something magic about the name in Hebrew. What it does say is that God has a name in every tongue, and it is sacred no matter how it is rendered. It is evident that there is no sin in rendering the divine name, *YHWH*, as "Lord," because the New Testament writers do so constantly. When citing Old Testament scriptures, they will render *YHWH*, with the Greek, *Kurios*, "Lord." In their day and among their readers, there was no argument as to who was "Lord."

"Out of the mouths of babes" is difficult, and there seems to be no help in other versions. I take this to mean that it is in utter simplicity that God silences the arguments of the enemies. As Paul put it:

> But God has chosen the foolish things of the world to confound the wise; and God has chosen the weak things of the world to confound the things which are mighty; And base things of the world, and things which are despised, has God chosen, yea, and things which are not, to bring to nought things that are: That no flesh should glory in his presence (1 Corinthians 1:27-29).

Psalm 9

*To the Chief Musician upon the death of the son,
A Psalm of David.*

I will praise you, O LORD, with my whole heart;
 I will show forth all thy marvelous works.
  I will be glad and rejoice in thee:
I will sing praise to your name, O thou most High.
3
When mine enemies are turned back,
 they shall fall and perish at thy presence.
For you have maintained my right and my cause;
 you sat in the throne judging right.
5
You have rebuked the nations,[1]
 you have destroyed the wicked,
  you have put out their name for ever and ever.
O enemy, destructions are come to a perpetual end:

---

[1] Hebrew: *Goy*, "nations," i.e., other nations.

20

you have destroyed cities;
their memorial is perished with them.

7

But the LORD shall endure for ever:
he has prepared his throne for judgment.
And he shall judge the world in righteousness,
he shall minister judgment to the people in uprightness.

9

The LORD also will be a refuge for the oppressed,
a refuge in times of trouble.
And they that know your name will put their trust in you:
for you, LORD, have not forsaken them that seek you.

11

Sing praises to the LORD, which dwelleth in Zion:
declare among the people his doings.
When he maketh inquisition for blood,
he remembereth them:
he forgetteth not the cry of the humble.

13

Have mercy upon me, O LORD; consider
my trouble which I suffer of them that hate me,
you that liftest me up from the gates of death:
That I may show forth all thy praise
in the gates of the daughter of Zion:
I will rejoice in thy salvation.

15

The heathen are sunk down in the pit that they made:
in the net which they hid is their own foot taken.
The LORD is known by the judgment which he executeth:
the wicked is snared in the work of his own hands.
(Meditation.) (Pause.)

17

The wicked shall be turned into hell,
and all the nations that forget God.
For the needy shall not always be forgotten:
the expectation of the poor shall not perish for ever.

19

Arise, O LORD; let not man prevail:
let the heathen be judged in thy sight.
Put them in fear, O LORD:
that the nations may know themselves to be but men.

The title of this song is "Upon *Muth-labben*" which apparently means, "to the tune of 'the death of the son,'" and I wonder if it is a reference to the death of Absalom. It is surely one of the most painful episodes in the life of David. And yet out of it arises a great Psalm of praise. It begins with four repetitions of "I will."

The first stanza contains two couplets. The first: "I will praise you." How? "I will show forth all thy marvelous works," the second line amplifying the first.

"That I may show forth your praise in the gates." The gates of a city were where business was transacted, where cases were tried by the elders of the city. This is tantamount to saying, "That I may *publicly* show forth your praise," in the public square, as it were. This, as opposed to praising God in the quiet of our prayer closet alone. We must not hide our faith, nor allow ourselves to be intimidated into silence.

Thinking this through, it becomes clear that Christians may, indeed they must, take their faith to the public square. This means writing, speaking, debating, if necessary, on the issues of the day. If a Christian has a firm, biblically based view of abortion, then it is right and proper for him to speak out in letters to the editor of his paper, in books, in discussions with friends and relatives, in town hall meetings, wherever the opportunity presents itself —including the ballot box. Intimidation of people who do not agree with our beliefs is wrong and counterproductive. Persuasion is one of the biblical arts that should be cultivated.

You have rebuked the nations,
you have destroyed the wicked,

22

The nations [1] are rebuked in the hope that they may turn and know Jehovah. The wicked, on the other hand, are deemed incorrigible and are simply destroyed.

"They who know your name": In Hebrew usage, "name" is a synonym for identity or reputation. It isn't merely a matter of pronouncing the name properly in Hebrew, but in knowing the identity of the true God. In English and American culture, when you speak of "God," it is assumed that you are speaking of the God of Abraham. In ancient Canaan, that was not the case. The landscape was littered with gods, but only one of them was *Yahweh*, Jehovah. Thus the Psalmist is speaking of "those who know who you are."

Psalm 10

Why do you stand afar off, O LORD?
Why do you hide yourself in times of trouble?
The wicked in his pride persecutes the weak:
Let them be taken in the devices that they have imagined.
For the wicked boasts of his heart's desire,
and blesses the covetous, whom the LORD abhors.
4
The wicked, through the pride of his countenance,
will not seek after God: God is not in all his thoughts.
His ways are always grievous;
your judgments are far above out of his sight:
as for all his enemies, he puffs at them.
He has said in his heart, I shall not be moved:
for I shall never be in adversity.
His mouth is full of cursing and deceit and fraud:
under his tongue is mischief and vanity.

---

[1] Hebrew: *Goy*, Gentiles or "heathen."

He sits in the lurking places of the villages:
in the secret places does he murder the innocent:
his eyes are secretly set against the helpless.
He lies in wait secretly as a lion in his den:
he lies in wait to catch the weak:
he catches the weak, when he draws him into his net.
He crouches, and humbles himself,
that the helpless may fall by his strong ones.
He has said in his heart, God has forgotten:
he hides his face; he will never see it.

12

Arise, O LORD; O God, lift up your hand:
forget not the afflicted.
Why does the wicked scorn[1] God?
he has said in his heart, that you will not require it.
You have seen it: for you behold mischief and spite,
to requite it with your hand:
the downtrodden commits himself unto you;
you are the helper of the bereaved.
Break the arm of the wicked and the evil man:
seek out his wickedness till you find none.

16

The LORD is King for ever and ever:
the aliens are perished out of his land.
LORD, you have heard the desire of the afflicted:
you wilt prepare their heart,
you wilt cause your ear to hear:
To judge the lonely and the oppressed,
that the man of the earth may no more oppress.

This Psalm would be a bass recitative in an oratorio, similar to "Why do the Nations?" from Handel's Messiah. It would resolve into an air with "the poor commits himself to you." But this is not

---

[1] Hebrew, *naats*: to scorn, blaspheme, despise.

a beautiful Psalm; it is downright disturbing. When the Bible speaks of "The Wicked," it is speaking of a singular evil. Think about the definition of The Wicked:

He condemns God.

He persecutes the poor.

His mouth is full of cursing, deceit, fraud, mischief and vanity.

He murders the innocent in secret places.

He catches the poor in a net.

This is not an ordinary sinner. This is evil personified. In the language of the day, it is a perfect description of Adolf Hitler, Joseph Stalin and Saddam Hussein, among others. Such terrible evil brings destruction on itself in the end, but the rise and fall are terrible.

"Why do you stand afar off O Lord?" This Psalm is a prayer, crying out to God on behalf of oppressed people who are being harmed by wicked men. Christians, even though sinners, do not stand afar off when a disaster strikes. They can be found everywhere, offering food, clothing and shelter to the afflicted. Then why should we stand idly by when the wicked are oppressing the poor and murdering the innocent? The very least we can do is to offer this prayer, to call God's attention to the works of evil men. Why does God stand afar off? Perhaps it is because Christians are not begging him to do something about the wicked.

Why would we not? Is it because we have dismissed the idea of real evil? Modern man seems to justify the wicked, alleging that he is that way because of something bad that happened to him. We think the wicked can be cured, and so are reluctant to pray against them. But this Psalm does not require that we pray against the evil by name. Only that we pray for God's judgment upon any man who would do these things.

Translation notes: The King James translators had some quirks. In this Psalm, they render two Hebrew synonyms with one English word, "poor," and then go on to toss "humble" into the equation. The Hebrew words in question are: *aniy*, (depressed or afflicted) and *chelaka* (dark, unhappy, wretched, miserable). The word, "poor," no longer carries the sense it did when the King James Version was produced. In this rendering, I have retained the sense of two synonyms rather than speak of them merely as "poor." These are weak, downtrodden, lowly, miserable, helpless people who are being crushed by wicked men.

The KJV choice of the word "heathen" is not bad, but I think "aliens" is more to the point. Israelite law made the stranger welcome if he became a God fearer. But if he persisted in being an alien, he had to go.[1]

Psalm 11

To the chief Musician, A Psalm of David

In the LORD I put my trust:
how say ye to my soul,
"Flee as a bird to your mountain.
For, lo, the wicked bend their bow,
they make ready their arrow upon the string,
that they may shoot from darkness[2]
at the upright in heart?"

3

If the foundations be destroyed, [3]
what can the righteous do?
The LORD is in his holy temple,
the LORD'S throne is in heaven:
his eyes behold, his eyelids try, the children of men.
The LORD tries the righteous: but the wicked
and him that loves violence his soul hates.
Upon the wicked he shall rain snares,

---

[1] See Ronald L. Dart, "Immigration Law," *Law and Covenant*, Wasteland Press, 2007, pp. 109 ff.

[2] KJV: "privily." Hebrew: *ophel*, "darkness."

[3] Figuratively, "If the moral and political support is pulled down."

> fire and brimstone, and an horrible tempest:
> this shall be the portion of their cup.
> For the righteous LORD loves justice;
> his countenance beholds the upright.

Another very heavy Psalm. Whoever put the collection together made no effort at balancing them out. But have you ever noticed how much music arises out of hard and desperate times? I guess when things are going good, men sing but don't compose a lot. It is when the going is bad that some of the greatest songs are written. It is true of music all the way from hymns in church to country music to folk songs.

"If the foundations be destroyed, what can the righteous do?" There are times when I feel that is what is going on around us. People are hacking away at the very foundations of our society. But against it all, God's eyes try the sons of men. He will judge. What can the righteous do? Once again I recall that the saints are called upon to pray that God will reward the wicked with justice. This is no idle call, but a serious responsibility. It may be that wicked men are succeeding because the righteous are not praying against them. It is, after all, spiritual warfare.

It doesn't seem very Christian to think that God hates any man, and yet the Psalm declares, "The wicked, and him that loves violence, the LORD hates." I think this is true anywhere that life is devalued.

Returning to the first stanza, notice the quotation marks. The statement is one of an enemy who is trying to make the psalmist afraid. It calls to mind an incident in the life of Nehemiah, a man sent back from Babylon to rebuild the walls of Jerusalem. He faced considerable opposition and had to endure spies as well. When he visited a man name Shemiah, he got a warning very similar to the one in this Psalm: "Let us meet in the house of God, inside the temple, and let us close the temple doors, because men are coming to kill you—by night they are coming to kill you" (Nehemiah 6:10 NIV).

Nehemiah saw through this immediately: "Should a man like me run away?" he replied. "Or should one like me go into the temple to save his life? I will not go!" He realized immediately that Shemiah had been hired by enemies to persuade him to do something wrong so they could accuse him. Nehemiah makes a good role model when people are trying to scare you. "Should a man like me run away?"

Psalm 12

To the Chief Musician upon the Lyre,
A Psalm of David.

Help, LORD; for the godly man ceases;
for the faithful fail from among the children of men.
They speak evil,[1] every one with his neighbour:
with flattering lips and with a double heart do they speak.
The LORD shall cut off all flattering lips,
and the tongue that speaks proud things:
Who have said, With our tongue will we prevail;
our lips are our own: who is lord over us?
5
For the oppression of the poor,
for the sighing of the needy,
now will I arise, saith the LORD;
I will set him in safety from him that puffs at him.
6
The words of the LORD are pure words:
as silver tried in a furnace of earth, purified seven times.
You shalt keep them, O LORD,
you shalt preserve them from this generation for ever.
8
The wicked walk on every side,
when the vilest men are exalted.

---

[1] Hebrew: *shav.* "Evil." NIV renders this, "Everyone lies to his neighbor."

It is awesome to consider a simple truism in this Psalm: "The words of the LORD are pure words: as silver tried in a furnace of earth, purified seven times. You shalt keep them, O LORD, you shalt preserve them from this generation for ever." Nearly 3000 years later, we still have those words preserved in the Bible. The care that has been taken in the preservation of the book is truly a testament to the faithfulness of God in spite of any perceived unfaithfulness of men.

Then there is that last verse: "The wicked walk on every side, when the vilest men are exalted." Within the last century, we have seen this repeated on a grand scale as low-life thugs and mobsters have gained control of the apparatus of governments. From Hitler to Stalin, to Saddam Hussein, they were all vile men who became exalted. And the wicked did indeed walk on every side.

Then, I hearken back to the first verse: "Help, LORD; for the godly man ceases; for the faithful fail from among the children of men." It calls to mind an image of a corrupt society where no one can speak truth any longer. In living memory, we have seen this again and again in totalitarian societies. In Hitler's Germany, for all that the world could see, no one stood in opposition to this evil man. One shudders to think that Hitler was actually elected by the people.

"For the oppression of the poor." As the Psalm uses the word, poor, it is not merely addressing the monetary status of a people. The word, *aniy*, denotes one who is depressed or afflicted. Poverty, defined in terms of income, has many causes. For some, it is a matter of mere indolence. These people are not oppressed, just lazy. But many are in poverty through no fault of their own. A family whose father is suffering from ALS is indeed poor in the biblical use of the word. These are the people who should have our help. Then there are those who are made poor by the oppression of greedy men and the criminal class. Their oppressors will draw the attention of the Almighty.

It occurs to me that the welfare state, though well intentioned, has the effect of putting the care of the afflicted in the hands of the impersonal state while relieving individuals of any responsibility to help. The net effect is to create a culture of dependency.

Psalm 13

To the chief Musician, A Psalm of David

How long will you forget me, O LORD? for ever?
How long will you hide your face from me?
How long shall I take counsel in my soul,
having sorrow in my heart daily?
How long shall mine enemy be exalted over me?
3
Consider and hear me, O LORD my God:
lighten mine eyes, lest I sleep the sleep of death;
Lest mine enemy say, I have prevailed against him;
and those that trouble me rejoice when I am moved.
5
But I have trusted in your mercy;
my heart shall rejoice in your salvation.
I will sing unto the LORD,
because he has dealt bountifully with me.

From the depths of despair, faith arises. There seems to be no logical connection between the despair of the first two verses and confidence of the last two—except the request that falls between them. So where does that faith come from? It seems to arise from a conscious decision to trust, no matter the outcome. As the three Hebrew children before the fiery furnace said, "Our God will deliver us. But even if he doesn't, know that we will not bow down to your idol." They placed their confidence in the righteousness of God. It turns out that faith is not merely a feeling. It is a conscious decision to trust, come hell or high water.

Psalm 14

To the chief Musician, A Psalm of David.

The fool has said in his heart, "There is no God."
They are corrupt, they have done abominable works,
there is none that does good.

2

The LORD looked down from heaven
upon the children of men,
to see if there were any
that did understand, and seek God.
They are all gone aside,
they are all together become filthy:
there is none that does good, no, not one.

4

Have all the workers of iniquity no knowledge
who eat up my people as they eat bread,
and call not upon the LORD?
There were they in great fear:
for God is in the generation of the righteous.

6

Ye have shamed the counsel of the poor,
because the LORD is his refuge.
Oh that the salvation of Israel were come out of Zion!
when the LORD bringeth back the captivity of his people,
Jacob shall rejoice, and Israel shall be glad.

It seems like such a pessimistic view of the world. And perhaps it was not a permanent view but what David saw at that time and that place. Yet Paul, in his letter to the Romans seems to put all mankind into the same bag. "What then?" he asks, "are we better than they?"

No, in no wise: for we have before proved both Jews and Gentiles, that they are all under sin; As it is written, There is none righteous, no, not one: There is none that understands, there is none that seeks after God. They are all gone out of the way, they are together become unprofitable; there is none that does good, no, not one (Romans 3:9-12).

It may seem pessimistic, but we have to accept that mankind, without a savior, fits the description. Without God we are lost and wandering in a fog.

In these days, when new books by atheists are appearing regularly, the words, "The fool has said in his heart, 'there is no God,'" are vivid. And why would intelligent men be so foolish? The psalmist offers the answer "They have done abominable works." Aggressive atheism, denial of God, arises from unrepented wrongdoing. Open minded agnosticism can be an honest response. Only when one feels condemned does open hostility toward God manifest itself.

A Christian, I think, has nothing to say to the atheist. That will have to be left to God. "Go from the presence of a foolish man," said Solomon, "when you perceive not in him the lips of knowledge" (Proverbs 14:7).

Psalm 15

A Psalm of David

LORD, who shall lodge in your tabernacle?
who shall reside in your holy hill?
He that walks uprightly, and works righteousness,
and speaks the truth in his heart.
He that backbites not with his tongue,
nor does evil to his neighbor,
nor even takes up a reproach against his neighbor.
In whose eyes a despicable person is despicable;
but he honors them that fear the LORD.

He that swears to his own hurt, and changes not.
He that puts not out his money to usury,
nor takes reward against the innocent.
He that does these things shall never be moved.

Who will live with God? The imagery draws from the nomadic culture of Israel in the desert. Among all their tents, there is the Tabernacle of God, his Pavilion. What kind of a man may lodge in God's tent? The answer lies in a striking description of the character of a good man. It is a call to humility for all of us, for there is no one who always measures up to these standards. That doesn't mean the standards aren't real, but that we must depend on God's grace to carry us over the rough spots.

Speaking the truth begins in the heart. Most of us lie to ourselves before we lie to others. Honest self appraisal, honest prayer to God, these things are a start on living an honest life.

The NIV has verse three correct: "and has no slander on his tongue, who does his neighbor no wrong and casts no slur on his fellow man." No man who is aware of his own shortcomings can lightly speak evil of another man.

"He that swears to his own hurt, and changes not." This is a man who keeps his word even when it hurts. The caution against usury arises from the law, and prohibits lending money on interest to the poor. It does not prohibit taking a return on investments. The last reference "does not accept a bribe against the innocent," presumes, of all things, jury duty.

It's all about character. Is it worth noting that there is nothing here about having the right doctrines, the right creeds? Perhaps he that "speaks the truth in his heart" is suggestive of that. But men of old knew only a fraction of what the apostles came to know about God. It is not so much about what you know. Gaps in our knowledge can be remedied. It is what we do that counts, and that is a matter of character.

Psalm 16

An engraving of David

Preserve me, O God: for in you do I put my trust.
O my soul, you have said to the LORD,
"You are my Lord: apart from you I have no good thing."
As for the saints that are in the earth,
they are the excellent, in whom is all my delight.

4

Their sorrows shall be multiplied
that hasten after another god:
their drink offerings of blood will I not offer,
nor take up their names into my lips.
Jehovah is the portion of mine inheritance
and of my cup: you maintain my lot.
The lines are fallen unto me in pleasant places;
yea, I have a goodly heritage.

7

I will bless the LORD, who has given me counsel:
my reins also instruct me in the night seasons.
I have set the LORD always before me:
because he is at my right hand, I shall not be moved.
Therefore my heart is glad, and my glory rejoices:
my flesh also shall rest in hope.

10

For you will not leave my soul in hell;
neither will you suffer your Holy One to see corruption.
You will show me the path of life:
in thy presence is fulness of joy;
at thy right hand there are pleasures for evermore.

To grasp the significance of the last stanza, one has to consider how Peter explained it on the day of Pentecost when the Holy Spirit fell on the disciples:

Because you wilt not leave my soul in hell, neither wilt you suffer thine Holy One to see corruption. You have made known to me the ways of life; you shalt make me full of joy with thy countenance. Men and brethren, let me freely speak unto you of the patriarch David, that he is both dead and buried, and his sepulchre is with us unto this day. Therefore being a prophet, and knowing that God had sworn with an oath to him, that of the fruit of his loins, according to the flesh, he would raise up Christ to sit on his throne; He seeing this before spake of the resurrection of Christ, that his soul was not left in hell, neither his flesh did see corruption (Acts 2:27-31).

There are two very important ideas in this short passage. One, David was a prophet. As one reads through the Psalms, this becomes important. Remembering that prophets sometimes required a minstrel in order to prophesy, we can see that David's poetry is more than a mere art form.

The other important idea is that the Psalm includes a prophecy of Christ's resurrection. Peter is explicit. David is still dead and buried. He has not been raised from the dead, but Jesus has been. "In your presence" and "at your right hand," are two powerful ideas coupled with a promise of eternal joy and delight. I recall what Paul said about this. "But as it is written, Eye has not seen, nor ear heard, neither have entered into the heart of man, the things which God has prepared for them that love him" (1 Corinthians 2:9).

Psalm 17

A prayer of David

Hear the right, O LORD, attend unto my cry,
give ear unto my prayer,
that goes not out of feigned lips.
Let my verdict come forth from your presence;
let your eyes behold the things that are equal.
You have proved my heart;
you have visited me in the night;
you have tried me, and shall find nothing;
I am purposed that my mouth shall not transgress.
4
Concerning the works of men,
by the word of your lips I have kept me
from the paths of the violent.
Hold up my goings in your paths, that my footsteps slip not.
I have called upon you, for you wilt hear me, O God:
incline your ear unto me, and hear my speech.
Show your marvelous loving-kindness,
O you who saves by your right hand
those who put their trust in you
from those who rise up against them.
8
Keep me as the apple of your eye,
hide me under the shadow of your wings,
From the wicked who oppress me,
from my deadly enemies, who compass me about.
They are enclosed in their own fat:
with their mouth they speak proudly.
They have now compassed us in our steps:
they have set their eyes bowing down to the earth;
Like as a lion that is greedy of his prey,

and as it were a young lion lurking in secret places.

13

Arise, O LORD, disappoint him, cast him down:
deliver my soul from the wicked, which is your sword:
From men which are your hand, O LORD,
from men of the world, which have their portion in this life,
and whose belly you fill with your hid treasure:
they are full of children,
and leave the rest of their substance to their babes.

15

As for me, I will behold your face in righteousness:
I shall be satisfied, when I awake, with your likeness.

David spoke of a prayer with no pretense. I think I have heard prayers that seem pretentious, prayers spoken in public to be seen and heard by men. One doesn't like to judge such things, so let us just accept that such prayers exist. Sometimes the person leading a group in prayer seems inclined to speak to the audience before him rather than to the Father.

The last verse of the Psalm is a stunning confirmation of the resurrection. It calls to mind something Paul wrote:

> But our citizenship is in heaven. And we eagerly await a Savior from there, the Lord Jesus Christ, who, by the power that enables him to bring everything under his control, will transform our lowly bodies so that they will be like his glorious body (Philippians 3:20-21 NIV).

And then there is this from John: "Beloved, now are we the sons of God, and it doth not yet appear what we shall be: but we know that, when he shall appear, we shall be like him; for we shall see him as he is" (1 John 3:2).

Could David have known these things when he wrote: "As for me, I will behold your face in righteousness: I shall be satisfied, when I awake, with your likeness"? I think he did, at some level. Although the word "satisfied" seems to be an understatement.

Psalm 18

To the chief Musician,
A Psalm of David, the servant of the LORD,
who spake unto the LORD *the words of this song*
in the day that the LORD *delivered him*
from the hand of all his enemies,
and from the hand of Saul. And he said:

𝕴 will love you, O LORD, my strength.
The LORD is my rock, and my fortress, and my deliverer;
my God, my strength, in whom I will trust;
my shield, and the horn of my salvation, and my high tower.
I will call upon the LORD, who is worthy to be praised:
so shall I be saved from mine enemies.

4

The sorrows of death compassed me,
and the floods of ungodly men made me afraid.
The sorrows of hell compassed me about:
the snares of death meet[1] me.

6

In my distress I called upon the LORD,
and cried unto my God:
he heard my voice out of his temple,
and my cry came before him, even into his ears.
Then the earth shook and trembled;
the foundations also of the hills moved
and were shaken, because he was furious.
There went up a smoke out of his nostrils,
and fire out of his mouth devoured:
coals were kindled by it.

---

[1] Hebrew, *quadam*, to project (oneself), i.e. precede; hence to anticipate, hasten, meet.

9

He bowed the heavens also, and came down:
and darkness was under his feet.
And he rode upon a cherub, and did fly:
yea, he did fly upon the wings of the wind.
He made darkness his secret place;
his pavilion round about him were dark waters
and thick clouds of the skies.
At the brightness that was before him
his thick clouds passed, hail stones and coals of fire.
The LORD also thundered in the heavens,
and the Highest gave his voice;
hail stones and coals of fire.
Yea, he sent out his arrows, and scattered them;
and he shot out lightnings, and discomfited them.
Then the channels of waters were seen,
and the foundations of the world
were discovered at thy rebuke, O LORD,
at the blast of the breath of thy nostrils.

16

He sent from above, he took me,
he drew me out of many waters.
He delivered me from my strong enemy,
and from them which hated me:
for they were too strong for me.
They prevented me in the day of my calamity:
but the LORD was my stay.

19

He brought me forth also into a large place;
he delivered me, because he delighted in me.
The LORD rewarded me according to my righteousness;
according to the cleanness of my hands
hath he recompensed me.
For I have kept the ways of the LORD,
and have not wickedly departed from my God.
For all his judgments were before me,
and I did not put away his statutes from me.

I was also upright before him,
and I kept myself from mine iniquity.
Therefore hath the LORD recompensed me
according to my righteousness,
according to the cleanness of my hands in his eyesight.

25

With the merciful thou wilt show thyself merciful;
with an upright man thou wilt show thyself upright;
With the pure thou wilt show thyself pure;
and with the adverse thou wilt show thyself adverse.

27

For thou wilt save the afflicted people;
but wilt bring down high looks.
For thou wilt light my candle:
the LORD my God will enlighten my darkness.
For by you I have run through a troop;
and by my God have I leaped over a wall.

30

As for God, his way is perfect:
the word of the LORD is tried:
he is a shield to all those that trust in him.
For who is God save the LORD?
or who is a rock save our God?
It is God that girdeth me with strength,
and maketh my way perfect.
He maketh my feet like hinds' feet,
and setteth me upon my high places.
He teacheth my hands to war,
so that a bow of steel is broken by mine arms.

35

Thou hast also given me the shield of thy salvation:
and thy right hand hath holden me up,
and thy gentleness hath made me great.
Thou hast enlarged my steps under me,
that my feet did not slip.
I have pursued mine enemies,
and overtaken them:

neither did I turn again till they were consumed.
I have wounded them that they were not able to rise:
they are fallen under my feet.
For thou hast girded me with strength unto the battle:
thou hast subdued under me those that rose up against me.

40

Thou hast also given me the necks of mine enemies;
that I might destroy them that hate me.
They cried, but there was none to save them:
even unto the LORD, but he answered them not.
Then did I beat them small as the dust before the wind:
I did cast them out as the dirt in the streets.
Thou hast delivered me from the strivings of the people;
and thou hast made me the head of the heathen:
a people whom I have not known shall serve me.
As soon as they hear of me, they shall obey me:
the strangers shall submit themselves unto me.
The strangers shall fade away,
and be afraid out of their close places.
The LORD liveth; and blessed be my rock;
and let the God of my salvation be exalted.

47

It is God that avengeth me,
and subdueth the people under me.
He delivereth me from mine enemies:
yea, thou liftest me up above those that rise up against me:
thou hast delivered me from the violent man.
Therefore will I give thanks unto you, O LORD,
among the heathen, and sing praises unto thy name.
Great deliverance giveth he to his king;
and showeth mercy to his anointed,
to David, and to his seed for evermore.

The early verses of this Psalm are a marvelous poetic description
of an aroused Father using every weapon in his arsenal to protect and
avenge his child. Historically speaking, there was nothing like this in

David's experiences. Unless it is somehow prophetic of the last days and the Messiah, it has to be seen as a good example of poetic imagery in describing God's intervention.

The stanza beginning at verse 25 is surprising. It seems to say that men often encounter a God who appears to match their personality. This may explain God's violence toward violent men. The KJV renders the Hebrew, *iqqesh*, as "froward," a middle English word that means "habitually disposed to disobedience and opposition." As it is used here, I take it to mean the man who is habitually in opposition, hence my choice of the word "adverse" to replace "froward." There are those who, no matter the issue, seem determined to oppose. Paul wrote to Timothy:

> And the servant of the Lord must not strive; but be gentle unto all men, apt to teach, patient, In meekness instructing those that oppose themselves; if God peradventure will give them repentance to the acknowledging of the truth (2 Timothy 2:24-25).

I take Paul to be referring to men who set themselves in opposition. And this calls to mind what may be a fundamental principle. Exposure of evil men to the Holy Spirit does not make them better. Rather it makes them worse. Being in the presence of the Spirit is a private hell for the man who is set in opposition. Thus when Peter quotes the Prophet Joel, "I will pour out my Spirit upon all flesh," it can be taken quite literally. But the Spirit may be destructive to some while it is empowering to others.

This is an idea I hope to return to later. The implications are far reaching. Watch for later editions of *Time with God, Reflections on the Psalms*.